I Feel Angry

Kelly Doudna

Published by SandCastle™, an imprint of ABDO Publishing Company, 4940 Viking Drive, Edina, Minnesota 55435.

Printed in the United States.

Photo credits: Adobe Image Library, Corel, Digital Stock, Digital Vision, MasterClips, PhotoDisc

Library of Congress Cataloging-in-Publication Data

Doudna, Kelly, 1963-
    I feel angry / Kelly Doudna.
       p. cm. -- (How do you feel?)
    Summary: Describes some things that can make you
angry and ways to deal with these feelings.
    ISBN 1-57765-187-1
    1. Anger in children--Juvenile literature.
  [1. Anger.] I. Title. II. Series: Doudna, Kelly,
1963- How do you feel?
  BF723.A4D68 1998
  152.4'7--dc21

98-26679
CIP
AC

The SandCastle concept, content, and reading method have been reviewed and approved by a national advisory board including literacy specialists, librarians, elementary school teachers, early childhood education professionals, and parents.

Let Us Know

After reading the book, SandCastle would like you to tell us your stories about reading. What is your favorite page? Was there something hard that you needed help with? Share the ups and downs of learning to read. We want to hear from you! To get posted on the Abdo Publishing Company Web site, send us email at:

sandcastle@abdopub.com

About SandCastle™
Nonfiction books for the beginning reader

- Basic concepts of phonics are incorporated with integrated language methods of reading instruction. Most words are short, and phrases, letter sounds, and word sounds are repeated.

- Readability is determined by the number of words in each sentence, the number of characters in each word, and word lists based on curriculum frameworks.

- Full-color photography reinforces word meanings and concepts.

- "Words I Can Read" list at the end of each book teaches basic elements of grammar, helps the reader recognize the words in the text, and builds vocabulary.

- Reading levels are indicated by the number of flags on the castle.

Look for more SandCastle books in these three reading levels:

Level 1 (one flag)	**Level 2** (two flags)	**Level 3** (three flags)

Grades Pre-K to K 5 or fewer words per page	**Grades K to 1** 5 to 10 words per page	**Grades 1 to 2** 10 to 15 words per page

When I feel angry, I make a face and stick out my tongue.

I feel better if I smile.

A happy smile helps my anger go away.

I feel angry when my brother will not let me sit on the couch.

I do not feel angry when Mom and I read a book together.

When I feel angry with someone at school, I might want to fight them.

If I count to ten, my anger fades.

Then I feel better.

I feel angry when my friend does not listen to me.

If we talk it out, we will find something that we have in common.

It is okay for me to feel angry.

Later, I will not feel angry.

Words I Can Read

Nouns

A noun is a person, place, or thing

anger (ANG-gur) pp. 7, 15
book (BUK) p. 11
brother (BRUHTH-ur) p. 9
couch (KOWCH) p. 9
face (FAYSS) p. 5
friend (FREND) p. 17

in common
 (IN KOM-uhn) p. 19
Mom (MOM) p. 11
school (SKOOL) p. 13
smile (SMILE) p. 7
ten (TEN) p. 15
tongue (TUHNG) p. 5

Pronouns

A pronoun is a word that replaces a noun

I (EYE) pp. 5, 7, 9, 11, 13,
 15, 17, 21
it (IT) pp. 19, 21
me (MEE) pp. 9, 17, 21
someone
 (SUHM-wuhn) p. 13

something
 (SUHM-thing) p. 19
them (THEM) p. 13
we (WEE) p. 19

Verbs

A verb is an action or being word

count (KOWNT) p. 15
do (DOO) p. 11

does (DUHZ) p. 17
fades (FAYDZ) p. 15

22

feel (FEEL) pp. 5, 7, 9, 11,
13, 15, 17, 21
fight (FITE) p. 13
find (FINDE) p. 19
go (GOH) p. 7
have (HAV) p. 19
helps (HELPSS) p. 7
is (IZ) p. 21
let (LET) p. 9
listen (LISS-uhn) p. 17

make (MAKE) p. 5
might (MITE) p. 13
read (REED) p. 11
sit (SIT) p. 9
smile (SMILE) p. 7
stick (STIK) p. 5
talk (TAWK) p. 19
want (WONT) p. 13
will (WIL) pp. 9, 19, 21

Adjectives

An adjective describes something

angry (ANG-gree)
pp. 5, 9, 11, 13, 17, 21
better (BET-ur) pp. 7, 15

happy (HAP-ee) p. 7
my (MYE) pp. 5, 7, 9, 15, 17
okay (oh-KAY) p. 21

Adverbs

An adverb tells how, when, or where
something happens

away (uh-WAY) p. 7
later (LATE-ur) p. 21
out (OWT) pp. 5, 19

then (THEN) p. 15
together
(tuh-GETH-ur) p. 11

Glossary

friend - Someone you like being with and know well.

smile - A widened mouth turned up at the corners. A smile shows that you are happy.

tongue - The movable piece of flesh in the mouth. It is used for tasting, swallowing, and talking.